A MAN
Pentheus, King of Thebes, determined to reign as supreme ruler of his city and refusing to bow to the divine power of Dionysus . . .

A WOMAN
Agave, mother of the King and leader of a band of women who worship the god of abandon and ecstasy . . .

A GOD
Dionysus, whose immortal spirit wreaks strange and terrible vengeance on mortal flesh . . .

THE BACCHAE

"Euripides does more than simply demarcate our mortal limitations. He intensifies our awareness of the mystery and immensity that lies beyond everyday experience. It is this awesome presence which palpably pervades *The Bacchae*."
    —from the Introduction by Michael Cacoyannis

MICHAEL CACOYANNIS—famed for his film of *Zorba the Greek* and his stage production of *The Trojan Women* —is the foremost interpreter of ancient Greek drama today. This brilliant new idiomatic translation of *The Bacchae* was widely acclaimed when Mr. Cacoyannis staged it for New York's Circle in the Square.

THE
BACCHAE

Euripides

TRANSLATED
AND WITH AN INTRODUCTION BY
Michael Cacoyannis

A MERIDIAN BOOK
NEW AMERICAN LIBRARY
A DIVISION OF PENGUIN BOOKS USA INC., NEW YORK
PUBLISHED IN CANADA BY
PENGUIN BOOKS CANADA LIMITED, MARKHAM, ONTARIO

Published by the Penguin Group
Penguin Books USA Inc., 375 Hudson Street,
New York, New York 10014, U.S.A.
Penguin Books Ltd., 27 Wrights Lane,
London W8 5TZ, England
Penguin Books Australia Ltd., Ringwood,
Victoria, Australia
Penguin Books Canada Ltd., 2801 John Street,
Markham, Ontario, Canada L3R 1B4
Penguin Books (N.Z.) Ltd, 182-190 Wairau Road,
Auckland 10, New Zealand

Penguin Books Ltd, Registered Offices:
Harmondsworth, Middlesex, England

The Bacchae previously appeared in a Mentor edition.

Library of Congress Catalog Card Number: 87-80754

First Meridian Printing, April, 1987

2 4 5 6 7 8 9 10

Printed in Canada

CONTENTS

INTRODUCTION

———◆◆◆———

A theatrical text is something of a literary paradox. It is written down, and yet it is not meant to be read. It is conceived in the form of words, and, if it survives, it does so because it can be read. Unlike a musical score, it is widely accessible in its written form; but like a musical score, it depends upon execution to summon it to life. This paradox is further compounded because only once they have proved themselves in performance do plays achieve literary status and acquire the dubious title of "classics"—dubious because of its highbrow and forbidding connotations. And when it comes to translating a classic, this proof in performance is in no way abridged, or predisposed in the translator's favor. Each new translation must stand or fall on its power to ignite the same first-degree involvement as the original, without interjecting its ghost.

To achieve this immediacy, the translator must keep close to the creative source, allowing himself the freedom that is needed to steer it into present life without betraying it. The two more obvious ways to fail are either to resort to that slavish respect for the academic form or letter which nails the play to some dead past, or to indulge in fanciful anachronisms, which cut it off from its roots and leave it stranded in some bizarre no-man's-land.

The inevitable losses in transplanting theatrical masterpieces are relative to the culture gap that separates us from them. In the case of, say, a Japanese or Chinese classical play, that gap may well be insurmountable for English-speaking audiences. With the ancient Greek tragedies, however, one can confidently claim that the very opposite holds true.

To begin with, the world they sprang from has shaped, sustained, and pervaded Western civilization down to the present day. Also, in purely theatrical terms, they have been an irresistible springboard for subsequent authors, with regard to form or content or both. Seneca, Shakespeare, Racine, Goethe, Brecht, T. S. Eliot, Anouilh, Sartre, MacLeish—to mention but a few—have all cast their bridges across time, connecting generation after generation with the one inexhaustible source.

If there is anything that separates people today from the prototypes themselves, it is not any real dimension of distance but a state of mind, a sort of misguided reverence that pushes the plays beyond the average person's imagined reach. The blame for this must go partly to the dissection of the Greek texts joylessly applied in the classroom and partly to the aura built around them by the appraisals of classical scholars, resourced from a lifetime's accumulation of specialized knowledge which I, for one, don't claim to share or propose to borrow for the purposes of this introduction.

Justified as that aura is, it carries with it one very

damaging assumption: that the plays cannot make their full impact unless we bring to them a certain amount of historical and literary hindsight, together with an appreciation of the principles governing the tragic-poetic form. This kind of elitist approach seems to me to go against the premise and purpose of theater, which not only takes ignorance in its stride, but steers it, through surprise and discovery, to its own desired ends.

Knowing the extent of popular participation in the festival performances of fifth-century-B.C. Greece, it would be unrealistic to presume that the authors—be it Aeschylus with his hieratic deployment of the chorus, Sophocles at his most inexorably tragic, or Euripides roaming freely across the spectrum of the human condition—aimed their plays at the literary elite of their day, any more than Shakespeare did in his. Or that they expected their audiences to judge their work by any historical yardstick or by their strict adherence to the tragic form rather than by the flow of emotion channeled through it.

When, as in certain periods of history, art creates its own tradition, providing the common channel for a massive flowering of individual expression, it is as futile to try to dissociate form from content as it is to explain their mysterious fusion, unique to all great works of art, making them run parallel with time. (With this difference: that theater, being plastically subject to constant renewal, is more evolutionary than most other arts which survive in their concrete, original identity.) In the same way that Impressionism and Surrealism have not blinded us to Botticelli, and that Mozart has not been silenced by electronic music, the Greek playwrights have not lost, as my experience has proved to me, any of their potential power to assail modern sensibilities. Especially is this true of Euripides, who drew on—and reshaped at will—history and legend in order to illustrate the evils that befoul human relationships and undermine social structures.

The past, whether illumined by historical evidence or veiled in mythology, has always been prime material for dramatists. In eras which have become landmarks of theatrical achievement, such as the Greek and the Elizabethan, the past predominated almost completely over contemporary events.

Historical fidelity was as little what they aimed for as was any betrayal of history by forcing the past into the straitjacket of another age. What they did create, through the interaction of past and present, was an elevated dimension of reality that stripped time of its mists, as well as of its more narrow and transitory associations.

When our heart leaps with terror as Oedipus staggers blind out of the palace or is wrenched by pity over Antony's and Cleopatra's deaths, it is not because of who they were in history or what they represented to Greek or Elizabethan audiences, but because the dramatist strikes at the roots of human emotion, where all people and all ages meet. If that cathartic power is not fully realized, it is, more often than not, because of our own overanxious tendency to "interpret" or "revive" the plays instead of trusting their autonomous clarity and purpose. Only plays that deal with passing social customs or conflicts risk dying with them.

The great authors of the past did not ignore the tide and signs of their times, but they knew the pitfalls of dramatizing history in the making. By choosing the historic parallel instead—and there is one for every situation—they could relate events to their full and final consequences. The sense of inevitability in Greek tragedy is rooted in this unassailable chain of cause and effect. Within it lies the only predictable link between present and future, enabling the authors to alert their public to the given realities, without dissipating emotional response with suspicions of moral or political bias. Of course, the cycle of human experience being one of recurring disaster, tragedy finds little scope for long-term optimism whichever way it looks —particularly when disaster takes the form of internecine war and overtakes the author in his own lifetime with such progressive and devastating momentum as it did in the case of Euripides.

He was around fifty when the Peloponnesian War broke out in 431 B.C., and by the time of his death some twenty-five years later, Athens was still locked and bleeding in its vicious grip. Had Euripides lived another two years to witness his city's final defeat from distant Macedonia, where he ended his days, the news would probably have pained him no more and no less than victory would have comforted him. Already in 416 B.C. he had said all there is to say about the immorality of war.

Appalled by the atrocities being committed by the Athenian military against their reluctant allies, he wrote *The Trojan Women*, which, as Edith Hamilton says in the introduction to her masterly translation of it, "is the greatest piece of antiwar literature there is in the world." Though the play is set hundreds of years earlier in Troy right after its fall, when Andromache cried out, "Greeks, you have found ways to torture that are not Greek," the message cannot have been lost on anyone in Euripides' audience. Nor is it lost—the word Greek being automatically transposed in the spectator's consciousness—on any audiences watching the play today.

Looking back on the catastrophic climax to that golden age whose spiritual conquests, spectacularly concentrated within a few decades, are paralleled only by the scientific advances of the last thirty years, one draws little encouragement. For humanity refuses still to heed Euripides' message—spelled out with prodigious versatility in *The Bacchae*—that all progress harnessed to the pursuit of absolute power engineers its own destruction.

That one wrenching cry of Andromache's quoted above is very revealing of the economy with which Euripides makes his points on multiple, and often paradoxical, levels. His unsparing indictment of Greek barbarism is instantly countered by his idealistic assessment of what Greece should stand for, and to some extent must have still stood for when he staged *The Trojan Women*. If not, he would have been shouted down by nationalistic indignation or, at least, been penalized after the fact. Evidently he had not altogether given up hope; which is not to say that he ever had too much hope or that he subsequently lost it. No artist combining the pragmatic wisdom with the lyrical imagination of Euripides is deluded by hope any more than he is dragged down by hopelessness. Otherwise he would not have gone on writing plays like *The Bacchae* and *Iphigenia in Aulis* (his two last) until his breath gave out.

His works, which are the best clue to his personality, encompass the full range of human hope, the positive and negative poles of its ephemeral yet resurgent tenacity, forever pitting itself against the stark confines of mortality. When his characters, in their arrogant or oblivious reliance on happiness, topple into darkness and all hope is banished from the stage, he regenerates it in the viewer by reversing the tables against the power of hopelessness to extinguish the spirit of man. Time and again in his later plays, his heroes, purged of hope and fear, march on through the ruins of their illusions with a fortitude that regards life and death as interchangeable and arms their resignation to or readiness for either. This fortitude, arrived at by different routes of despair, manifests itself in individual ways, ranging from the searing confrontation of guilt in oneself (Electra, Orestes) to the noble forgiveness of it in others (Iphigenia) and from resigned endurance (Hecuba, Cadmus) to cosmic defiance (Agave). But in each instance it elevates those who possess it into a state of rarefied emotional honesty, wisdom, or courage that lays bare the futility of man's struggle for self-assertion in all sectors of life—private and public, material and spiritual—of which war is the ultimate, totally self-defeating expression. So too, by the distance they gain from it all, once released from the bondage of their own vanity, Euripides makes them stand out like indestructible links in the chain of mortality's survival in time. He has Hecuba say as much in an extraordinary passage of historical illumination:

And yet—had God not bowed us down,
not laid us low in dust,

> none would have sung of us or told our wrongs
> in stories men will listen to forever.
>
> [*The Trojan Women*]

Euripides' abhorrence not only of war but of everything that leads up to it, polluting our lives, is a recurrent motif in his plays. This may seem strange for someone who grew up in a society thriving on the glory of its recent victories against the Persian invaders. Unlike Aeschylus, who actually fought at the battle of Marathon, and Sophocles, who was his senior by some fifteen years, he was far too young to have been bitten by any patriotic fervor. (If we are to credit the story that in his early childhood he watched the battle of Salamis from his father's country house on that island, the sight and roar of clashing ships and drowning men could well have been traumatic to one too young to understand the reasons for such violence. This may account for his lifelong habit of withdrawing to the solitude of a cave on Salamis and gazing out to sea, though arguably the story may have originated because of it.)

In any case, he was clear enough on the painful but honorable necessity of defensive war:

> This truth stands firm. The wise will fly from war.
> But if war comes, to die well is to win
> the victor's crown.
>
> [Cassandra, in *The Trojan Women*]

Evidently, pride he took in his country's heroic stand against the Persians, but less for the military glory stemming from its victories than for the spirit which, win or lose, ennobles all those who resist unprovoked aggression, for they are, in effect, fighting against war itself and for what to Euripides was the most precious and precarious possession of all, peace—precarious because the aftermath of victory, however nobly won, too often corrupts with delusions of power and national supremacy, fostering the seeds of oppression and armed conflict.

To the humane eye of Euripides, the danger signs in Athenian society, set on its isolated and spiraling course of discovery and progress at the expense of other, simpler human values (wherein, as he says in *The Bacchae*, lies the only measure for happiness in its day-to-day fragility), must have been plain as to few others. He expressed his concern by exposing the evil roots of social inequality, racism, political ambition, spiritual arrogance, religious dogmatism. And if his voice was jarring to the smug ears of his critics, in retrospect it must have soon sounded prophetic enough. The posthumous recognition accorded him in war-racked Athens comes into eloquent contrast with the few festival prizes he won in his lifetime (four as opposed to Aeschylus' thirteen and Sophocles' twenty or more). A chronicler reports:

> Hearing that Euripides was dead, Sophocles brought on his chorus and actors without their crowns and himself put on mourning. And the people wept.

If proof is needed that it is the critics and not the artists who are the false prophets of their times, it is furnished by the tears that endorsed his immortality.

Clearly, whatever the reasons that drove Euripides to leave Athens and settle in Macedonia at so advanced an age, the large public accepted them without resentment or bitterness. When one considers the inevitably intolerant mood of the embattled Athenians, this demonstration of their respect belies the theory that his move to the court of King Archelaus might have been intended or regarded (except by his confirmed enemies) as an open snub to the city which had maligned and humiliated him. Nor can one look for clues in the picture drawn of him by contemporary gossip, for it adds up to little more than an admission of ignorance about the real man. It is the picture of one aloof, unconvivial, of comfortable means but unhappily married; of one who, unlike his eminent fellow tragedians, took no part in public affairs; of one who was interested in the ideas of others (particularly Anaxagoras, Protagoras, and Socrates, with whom he socialized in the narrowest of circles) but refused allegiance to any philosophic school or movement.

Given this image, it is hardly surprising that the intellectual establishment of his day went out of its way to deride him for pomposity, muddled thinking, misogyny, religious disrespect, and lack of patriotic commitment. What is more disconcerting is that the bias which blinded Euripides' critics to his true intentions and to the honesty of his unconventional choices lingered on through the centuries in the minds of those scholars who, in their pedantic regard for historical testimony, have sought to justify the reasons for his recorded unpopularity.

It takes perhaps a certain amount of artistic empathy

to assess not only the unfair price paid by solitary and nonconformist artists but their ability to cope with the inevitable hurt. Had Euripides not been able to rise above his critics, it is highly unlikely that he would have waited so long before turning his back on Athens. Besides, the unabated pace of his output (reaching a total of ninety-two plays, of which nineteen survive) indicates both his resilience to criticism and the public's continuing interest in his work. But after twenty-three years of war, he could do little more than watch the steady corrosion of democratic freedoms. Even at the best of times, an invitation by a friendly and respected patron of the arts like Archelaus would have been tempting; nor was he setting any precedent by making such a move (Aeschylus had died in Sicily). And if the respite and creative stimulus offered by the peace and beauty of Macedonia do not seem justification enough, any possible motives of protest which we might read into his voluntary exile would be more compatible with his pacifist ideals than with the pettier personal considerations attributed to him.

The unending fascination with Euripides' personal life is as direct a comment as any on the intriguing and unorthodox nature of his work. The gratuitous assumptions about the former are reflected in the arbitrary, and often antithetical, evaluations of the latter. Characteristically, the quality which makes him so arresting and accessible to modern audiences—his psychological exploration of character—is regarded by some scholars as a rather dubious tragic virtue. While it steps up emotional involvement, they argue, it traps him into incongruities of style and realistic excesses.

There is little doubt that the rigidity of the traditional conventions was too restricting for Euripides. His discomfort at being stuck with them is particularly evident in those plays in which his focus on the dramatic situation is arbitrarily broken by the intrusions of an extraneous chorus. (In *Iphigenia in Aulis*, for instance. Respect him as I do, in transposing that tragedy to film, I had to dispense with it.) Yet even then, he commands our attention with lyrical passages of extraordinary subtlety and beauty. Conversely, few tragedies integrate the chorus as effectively as those with the chorus named in the titles (*The Suppliants, The Trojan Women, The Bacchae*).

Uneven though the body of his work admittedly is— ragged at its worst, masterly at its best—its range and provocative diversity show that he was not one to balk at the prospect of raising a few eyebrows with his revolutionary departures. With equal regularity he knocked gods and kings off their pedestals and raised peasants and slaves to the topmost rank of natural nobility. He introduced all kinds of daring scenic devices (as for his *deus ex machina* apparitions) and mixed drama with wit (ranging from sophisticated irony to the grotesque) and earthy wisdom with metaphysical phenomena. We encounter such innovations in many of his plays but never so magically orchestrated as in his incontestable masterpiece, which is *The Bacchae*.

For all his defiant questioning of social, moral, or religious values, at the heart of the Euripidean universe lies intellectual humility, honed by a restless and ferocious intelligence. His mind struck out in all directions and often bounced back with the warning, re-verberated throughout *The Bacchae*, that

> Knowledge is not wisdom.
> A knowing mind that ignores its own limits
> has a very short span.

Pronouncements of this kind, made in an age when knowledge was the key to all, were hardly likely to be accepted at their philosophical face value. Many latter-day scholiasts have classified him as a skeptic, others as a rationalist, an agnostic, or a precursor of existentialism. But no amount of sophisticated argument can force his sensibility into any one philosophical pigeonhole which, while revealing part of the truth, may be challenged on the evidence of the truth it obscures.

The seeming contradictions in Euripides are like the contradictions of life itself—as complacently ignored or miscalculated by man as they are consistent with the mysterious and implacable laws which govern his existence. To project that discrepancy, Euripides juxtaposes man's subjective outlook with a dispassionate assessment of its endemic fallibility. By identifying with his characters' passions and pursuits on one level while exposing the perilous insecurity of the man-made order by which, and within which, they live on another, he traces the tragic course of human destiny. For trapped as his heroes are in their oblivious and arrogant world, they become by their actions the instruments of doom as well as its victims; victims because their self-created doom invariably catches them off their guard, in cruel and, to them, unpredictable ways.

This elusive element of unpredictability has led to some curious interpretations. It has been claimed that in his skeptical attitude toward the gods, Euripides had to relinquish the concept of Fate, which, being foreordained by divine will, lends Greek tragedy its unique dimension of inevitability. And that, for lack of anything better, he had to settle for Chance or Luck as the force which rules over men's lives, haphazardly and unpredictably. This strikes me as confusing the issues in all possible directions, by narrowing his intentions down to the subjective level of his less-enlightened characters. Reading his plays in cold print, one can, no doubt, pick out the odd phrase that refers to Chance in its popularly accepted sense. But one can quote twice as many in Shakespeare, without feeling constrained to define his philosophy by them.

What indeed appears as unpredictable to the men and women in Euripides may evoke our compassion against the dictates of our reason, but it cannot obscure the pattern which paves the way to their doom. Though structured around a less monolithic concept of Fate (integrating human responsibility in the way we have seen), there is nothing fortuitous about this pattern —except for calculated dramatic effect—either in its stage-by-stage progression or in its overall tragic view of life. If anything, being less strictly circumscribed by religious convention, what it loses in linear unity or hieratic stature it gains in psychological and philosophic conviction.

Not that Euripides goes out of his way to indulge in philosophical abstractions. He builds his arguments by point and counterpoint, making a fair case for all his characters, however bigoted (the Agamemnon-Menelaus confrontation in *Iphigenia in Aulis* is an outstanding example). And he never pursues ideas beyond their natural "span" by trying to define the indefinable. Even when he makes the gods materialize, there is a startling physical immediacy about his plays, resulting from his anatomical observation of human behavior and heightened by his vivid and prodigious evocation of the beauty and cruelty of Nature. In *The Bacchae* particularly, he crowds the stage with towering mountains, racing torrents, and forests teeming with wild fauna, creating a perfect backdrop for the play's orgiastic exuberance.

But in focusing on the finite world of our perceptions and the contradictory forces within it, Euripides does more than simply demarcate our mortal limitations. He intensifies our awareness of the mystery and immensity that lie beyond everyday experience. It is this awesome presence which palpably pervades *The Bacchae* and gives it its metaphysical dimension. It also provides the key to the range and substance of his religious credo, which has been the subject of great controversy.

Man, he repeatedly tells us, is flawed by reason of his mortality. His attempts to define God are inevitably scaled to the measure of his hopes, fears, and needs. The closer he fashions his gods to his own image, the more reassuring they are in their immortality. These gods Euripides not only regards with undisguised skepticism, but frequently represents in a cruelly realistic dimension, variously maneuvering and being maneuvered by men's passions.

In *The Bacchae*, however—at least before its denouement—his aims in making Dionysus pivotal to the action are broader and more complex. Theatrically, his physical incarnation gains credibility by the fact that among the gods, he is the one legitimately closest to us, representing Nature in all its elemental aspects, around us as well as within us. More significantly, he is also an antitraditional god in that he heralds the disintegration into anarchy of any social or religious culture, which, in its moral intransigence and dogmatic application of law and order, defies change.

Change, in this instance, comes—as it often does to this day—from the mountainous heart of Asia, in the form of the Dionysiac or Bacchic cult, preaching freedom of mind and body. (This was before Dionysus degenerated into the image eventually handed down to us by the Romans—a fat, licentious Bacchus, god of wine and nothing more. The Romans failed to grasp Euripides' message about the arrival of new religions from the East to sweep away the old, made all the more poignant by the symbolic similarities between Dionysus and Christ, sons of God and a virgin, offering the blessing of their blood as wine.)

But Euripides' faith was no more vested in Dionysus than in Zeus, his father. It reached out to the infinity beyond and the invisible powers of universal justice and balance, invoked by the chorus of *The Bacchae* and Hecuba in *The Trojan Women*.

> Holiness, power all transcending,
> soaring higher than the Gods
> yet floating down on golden wings
> to touch the earth . . .

[The Bacchae]

O thou who dost uphold the world,
whose throne is high above the world,
thou, past our seeking hard to find, who art thou?
God or Necessity of what must be,
or Reason of our reason?
Whate'er thou art, I pray to thee,
seeing the silent road by which
all mortal things are led by thee to Justice.

[*The Trojan Women*]

To the extent that Dionysus is the instrument of this Justice, Euripides presents him as a necessary and positive force. But at a crucial point in the play, the chorus tells us: "Justice is balance." And this balance is what the new cult—being imperfectly conceived and practiced by man—ultimately cannot keep. As it tips over into excess, Euripides makes Dionysus withdraw into the nebulous area of unreality, equating him with all two-dimensional and expendable deities. True to pattern, he thus reverses the coin and affirms his humanism, by raising Agave—purged by terror and suffering—to a state of higher consciousness.* Her challenging of the punishing gods—for being prey to mortal passions—elicits from Dionysus merely religious sophistry:

So it was ordained from the beginning
by the almighty father, Zeus.

* The loss of a considerable number of lines of manuscript covering Agave's transition from the horror and heartbreak of discovery to her rejection of Dionysus is as crucial as it is tantalizing. In filling in the gap, I departed considerably from the standard practice of borrowing from *Christus Patiens*, a twelfth-century patchwork of Euripidean plays. To justify my audacity, I can only

Putting my thoughts on paper, I have become increasingly aware of one simple fact. It is the same that I expressed after first coming to grips with *The Bacchae* in its proper setting, the living stage. This was in 1978 at the Comédie Française. In my note for the program I wrote, "This is a play which like life itself defies analysis."

After directing it for a second time, in my own translation, at New York's Circle in the Square in 1980, I reiterated this opinion. The play defeats analysis not so much because I find any of it unclear in its step-by-step construction or exposition of ideas, but because the simplicity of its parts belies the enormity of the whole. Point after point, as it hits home, sets off repercussive associations, like concentric circles endlessly overtaking each other, forming and reforming into new yet dynamically balanced patterns. To keep track of them, much less to define them rigidly, is not merely impossible. It is more than Euripides intended or was himself even aware of. To say this is not to diminish his genius. It is to recognize it.

---

plead my very strong feeling—part intuition, part logic—that Euripides could hardly have plunged Agave into such unrelieved self-pity and lamentation without planting the seeds of her stark and defiant resolution to live out her life without God. Also, to bridge the action back to the existing text, I wrote a short chorus commenting on the benevolence and cruelty of the natural forces represented by Dionysus and eliminated several verses of his ensuing speech, because of their obscure mythological associations.

A NOTE ON
THE TRANSLATION

—◆◆—

Like all modern translators of Greek drama, I did not
attempt the impossible: that is, to reproduce either the
same number of verses or the strict metric pattern of
the original. My concern was that the text have the
right emotional flow and rhythm, and that it sound
convincing in the mouths of the characters. I divided
the lines, as much by calculation as by instinct, to aid
comprehension and to show how actors might render
them. This is particularly evident in the passages of
the chorus. Each has a very distinctive poetic texture
and dramatic flavor. I hope that the way the verses are
set out both clarifies the meaning and gives an indica-
tion of music and mood. To render dramatic movement through sound is essential in the performance of
Greek tragedy, but it is not always easy to explain this
on paper.

THE
BACCHAE

Euripides

DRAMATIS PERSONAE

——◆·◆——

DIONYSUS, also called Bromius and Bacchus
CHORUS OF ASIAN BACCHAE, followers of Dionysus
TEIRESIAS, a blind seer
CADMUS, former king of Thebes
PENTHEUS, his grandson and present king
A GUARD
A HERDSMAN
A MESSENGER
AGAVE, daughter of Cadmus and mother of Pentheus

SCENE

— ❖ —

Before the king's palace in Thebes. Across from the
gates, in the downstage area, is the tomb of Semele
(DIONYSUS' mother), half-ruined and thickly covered
with vine. Every now and then, a strand of smoke
rises up out of the stones. Access to the city can be
gained on all sides. Upstage left is the way to Mount
Cithaeron.

There is a crash of thunder, followed by an eerie
stillness, accentuated by the rustling of leaves. Out of
it grows a distant drone of women's voices, and
DIONYSUS appears.

He carries a thyrsus (a stick twined with ivy), and
his scant dress, draped with animal skin, suggests the
Orient. His flowing blond hair, cascading around his
shoulders, and his lithe, smooth-skinned limbs com-
plement the feline, almost feminine grace of his move-
ments.

DIONYSUS

I, Dionysus, son of Zeus, am back in Thebes.
I was born here, of Semele, daughter of Cadmus,
blasted from her womb by a bolt of blazing thunder.
Why am I here? A god in the shape of a man,
walking by the banks of Ismenus, the waters of Dirce?
Look out there! That house in ruins,
still smoking, smoldering still with unquenchable
    flame,
is my mother's monument,
her thunder-dug grave,
undying evidence of spiteful Hera's rage.
Let's give some praise to Cadmus,
who turned it into consecrated ground, a living temple
that I shrouded with clustering vine.
I left behind the gold-abounding lands
of Lydia and of Phrygia,
Persia's sun-beaten plains and Bactria's giant walls,
crossing the winter-scorched earth of the Medes
and the length of happy Arabia, in short,
all Asia down to its shimmering seashores

[5]

where Greeks and barbarians freely mingle
in teeming, shapely-towered cities,
and here I am. In Greece.
This is the first of its cities I visit.
I danced my way throughout the East,
spreading my rituals far and wide—a God
made manifest to men.
Of all Greek cities, Thebes is the one I chose
to rouse into a new awareness,
dressing Greek bodies in fawnskins,
planting the thyrsus in Greek hands,
my ivied spear.
My mother's sisters—
were there ever more unsisterly sisters—
gossiped that this Dionysus was no child of Zeus,
that Semele having slept with some man
proceeded—on Cadmus' cunning advice—
to attribute her sinful conception to God.
No wonder Zeus struck her dead, they would prattle,
taking a lover and brazenly lying!
Well! These sisters, all three,
I've stung into a frenzy and steered them
from their homes into the mountains,
where I left them raving. Complete of course
with full orgiastic trappings. What is more,
all the women of Thebes, but all,
I've sent stampeding out of doors. They're up there
        now,
milling with Cadmus' daughters under the fresh-
        smelling pines
or high upon the rocks. This town must learn,
even against its will, how much it costs
to scorn God's mysteries and to be purged.

So shall I vindicate my virgin mother
and reveal myself to mortals as a God,
the son of God.
Now hear this.
King Cadmus has conferred the powers of his throne
with all attending honors on his grandson, Pentheus.
This God-fighting upstart snubs me; banishes my name
from public sacrifice and private prayer.
He'll soon find out, and every Theban with him,
whose birthright is divine and whose is not.
Once that score is settled, I'll move on
to manifest myself in other lands. But should this town,
in blind anger, take up arms to drive my Bacchae from
        the hills,
I'll give them war,
leading my women's army to the charge.
To this end,
I have disguised myself as a mortal,
adopting the ways and features of a man.

> [*The* CHORUS OF ASIAN BACCHAE *appears during
> the following lines, coming from the same direc-
> tion as* DIONYSUS. *They wear fawnskins and gar-
> lands of ivy leaves and flowers twined around
> their necks. Apart from the thyrsus, several carry
> skin drums of various shapes, which they beat as
> the action—or their emotion—requires*]

You! Women of Tmolus, Lydia's towering mountain,
my band of initiates, you,
whom I unplucked from your primitive lands
to be my road companions and my friends,
raise up your native Phrygian drums
that pulse to rhythms that are mother earth's and mine.

[7]

Surround the royal home of Pentheus with your beat
and turn the city out to see. Meanwhile,
I'll make my way to those Cithaeron slopes
that seethe with Theban Bacchae
and join their dance.

> [DIONYSUS *goes off toward Mount Cithaeron to a*
> *rising crescendo of drumbeats*]

CHORUS

Out of the heart of Asia
down from the sacred heights of Tmolus
have I come. For the God—
Bromius, Bacchus, Dionysus—
fatigue is sweet to the limbs,
and effortless effort the trek
when you are shouting with joy.
Who is there in the street? Who?
Who is lurking in the house? Stand still,
stand back and hold your breath,
while I chant a prayer immemorial,
in praise of Dionysus.

Oh, happy the man who, blessed by his knowledge
     of God,
discovers purity.
Who opens his heart to togetherness.
Who joins in mountain-dancing
and sacred cleansing rituals. He,
who sanctifies the orgies of Cybele,
the mother of fertility,
waving the thyrsus high,
crowning his head with ivy,
in honor of Dionysus.

[8]

Go, Bacchae, go, go, go! Bring
God's godly son—our Bromius—
down from the Phrygian hills
out into the spacious streets of Greece—
the home of Dionysus.
Him,
whom his mother carried
to premature and painful birth
when in a crash of thunder
she was death-struck by a fiery bolt.
But quicker than death,
Zeus swept him up and plunged him
into a makeshift womb—
secure from Hera's eyes—
in the thick of his thigh,
stitched with stitches of gold.
As time ripened into fate
he delivered the bull-horned God
and crowned him with a crown of serpents.
Thus was created the custom
for thyrsus-carrying maenads
to twine snakes in their hair.

Oh, Thebes, Semele's nurse,
crest your walls with ivy.
Burst into greenness, burst
into a blaze of bryony,
take up the bacchanalian beat
with branches of oak and of fir,
cover your flesh with fawnskin
fringed with silver-white fleece
and lifting the fennel,

touch God
in a fit of sanctified frenzy.
Then all at once, the whole land will dance!
Bacchus will lead the dancing throngs to the mountain,
the mountain,
which is home to that mob of women,
who rebelled against shuttle and loom
answering the urge
of Dionysus.

Oh holy heights of Crete
cradling the caves of the Curetes
where Zeus was born.
There, the triple-crested Corybantes
traced in vibrant skin
the circle of my joy.
They married its percussive strength
to the wailing sweetness of flutes,
then put it into Rhea's hands
to draw the earth-beat out
and make it throb in Bacchic song.
In time, the frenzied Satyrs
from the Mother-Goddess stole the drum
and struck up dances for the feasts,
held evey second year,
to honor and give joy to Dionysus.

How sweet to the body, when
breaking loose from the mountain revels
you collapse to the ground in a fawnskin
after hunting the goat.

How sweet the kill—
the fresh-smelling blood—
the sacramental relishing
of raw flesh . . .

Oh Asia, great mother,
my distant mountain home!
How the mind races back
to those peaks that clang in glory,
of Bromius, evoë . . .
Your ground flows with milk,
flows with wine, flows with nectar from the bees.
Like smoke from a Syrian incense,
the fragrant God arises with his torch of pine.
He runs, he dances in a whirl of flame,
he rouses the faithful
crazing their limbs with his roar,
while he races the wind,
his soft hair streaming behind.
And his call resounds like thunder:
"Go, my bacchae, go!
Let Tmolus with its golden streams
reverberate with songs of Dionysus,
and the vibrant crash of drums.
Sing out in joy
with loud Phrygian cries,
while the holy sweet-throated flute
climbs the holy scale and the scaling maenads climb
up the mountain,
the mountain."

It is then, that a girl like me
knows happiness. When she is free,

like a filly playfully prancing
around its mother,
in fields without fences.

[*The* CHORUS *withdraws silently to one side as*
TEIRESIAS *enters, ivy-crowned and with a fawnskin over his shoulders. His festive dress seems
oddly out of step with his old age and ascetic
bearing. Being blind, he carries a staff, tipped
with ivy leaves*]

TEIRESIAS

Who is at the gates? Go call Cadmus out,
Cadmus, son of Agenor who sailed from distant Sidon
to build the fortress walls of Thebes.
Just say Teiresias wants him. He already knows
why I am here. We made a pact, he and I
—old me with him who is older still—
to take up the thyrsus, put on our fawnskins
and top them with garlands of twirling ivy.

[CADMUS *comes out of the palace, forestalling the*
GUARD *who is about to call him. Like* TEIRESIAS,
*he is very old and looks equally incongruous in
his Dionysiac garb*]

CADMUS

Dear friend! I knew you were here by the sound of
        your voice,
the voice of wisdom that makes a wise man welcome.
I come to you ready, dressed to please God,
as indeed I should, for is not Dionysus
my own daughter's son? Now that mankind has seen
        his light
we must do our very best to exalt him. So!

Where should we dance? Where do we fling a leg
and toss our grizzly heads? It is for you
to guide me, Teiresias, though you be as ancient as I.
Initiation is your job. I'll never tire night or day,
of thumping the ground with my thyrsus. Oh, what bliss
to forget how very old one is!

TEIRESIAS

You speak the way I feel. Young again
and just as tempted to try a little dance.

CADMUS

You don't think that a carriage—for the mountains—
would be more sensible?

TEIRESIAS

Indeed no.
That would diminish our respect for the God.

CADMUS

Then let me, being older, be your nursemaid, old man.

TEIRESIAS

We'll let the God lead us. No need to exert ourselves.

CADMUS

Are we the only men in Thebes to dance to Bacchus?

TEIRESIAS

The only ones with healthy minds. The rest are sick.

CADMUS

We are wasting time. Here, take my hand.

TEIRESIAS

And you take mine. There, get a good grip.

CADMUS

After all, who am I, a mortal, to put down the Gods?

TEIRESIAS

Only fools play speculative games with the Gods.
But we, we cling to what we learned from our fathers,
beliefs that are as old as time and as immune
to the onslaught of words, no matter how clever the
theory,
how complex the argument, the human mind can
invent.
No doubt people will say it's a disgrace—
an old man like me, dancing, with ivy in my hair.
Well, let them! Who ever heard of God
segregating the young from the old,
saying these should dance and these should not?
He expects to be honored by one and all,
not by degrees or in sections.

CADMUS

Teiresias, you cannot see the light
so let my words enlighten you.
I see Pentheus, the son of Echion, to whom
I've handed over all powers of state,
rushing toward the palace.
How wild he looks! There's something in the wind.
Let's hear.

[PENTHEUS *bursts onto the stage, accompanied by
his military guard. He is about the same age as
Dionysus, whom he resembles in looks but little
else. Austerely dressed, he is as angular in his
masculinity as he is strident when, as now, he is
in a rage. He does not notice* CADMUS *and*
TEIRESIAS, *who have crept out of his way.*]

[14]

What an unholy mess!

No sooner does one venture on a journey,

than rumor plagues the town and things get out of
    hand.

Our women, I am told, have left their homes,

in a religious trance—what travesty!—

and scamper up and down the wooded mountains,
    dancing

in honor of this newfangled God, Dionysus,

whoever he may be.

In the middle of each female group

of revelers, I hear,

stands a jar of wine, brimming! And that taking turns,

they steal away, one here, one there, to shady nooks,

where they satisfy the lechery of men,

pretending to be priestesses,

performing their religious duties. Ha!

That performance reeks more of Aphrodite than of
    Bacchus.

The ones I have already caught are being guarded,
    manacled

and safely locked behind bars. The others, still at large,

I shall thrash out of the mountains, the lot,

including my own mother, Agave, and her sisters

Ino and Autonoe, I'll clap them into irons, I swear,

I'll put a stop to this orgiastic filth!

The other news

is that some stranger has arrived in town,

a sorcerer from Lydia, a conjurer of sorts,

with golden scented hair tumbling down to his
    shoulders,

a skin that glows like wine, and eyes
that promise Aphrodite's secret charms.
He spends his nights and days with girls, I hear,
enticing them with his Bacchic witchcraft.
Just let me catch him hanging round these streets,
and his thyrsus-tapping, hair-tossing days are over.
His body will be looking for his head.
He is the one who spreads the tale
that Dionysus is a God,
hatched from the thigh of Zeus,
in which he had been sewn. As if we didn't know
the truth about Dionysus and his liar of a mother,
both of them burned to a cinder by a bolt of flame
hurled by Zeus, her so-called bedmate.
Foul-mouthed foreigner! His tongue will earn him
the foulest punishment my power can pronounce.
Death by hanging! Let him be warned, whoever he
    may be.

    [*He turns to go and sees* TEIRESIAS *first, then*
    CADMUS]

Ye Gods! What new marvel have we here? Teiresias,
the prophet, all dolled up in spotted skins!
And my mother's father—how grotesque—
playing bacchant with his wand and all!
I am ashamed, sir! How can a man so old
be so devoid of sense!
Take off that ivy, will you?
And drop that thyrsus. Now! Do you hear?
This is all *your* doing, Teiresias! Using him,
to launch this new God to the masses.
Convenient, isn't it? Give religion a boost

and prophets grow fat, raking in the profits
from reading the stars and fire-magic.
You can thank your white hairs for being here and not
    in prison,
chained with those raving females; just the place for
    frauds
who encourage their obnoxious rituals. Take my word,
when women are allowed to feast on wine, there is no
    telling
to what lengths their filthy minds will go!

CHORUS

The blasphemy of the man! Who are you
to think you can insult the Gods? Or Cadmus,
who sowed the seed from which you sprang?
Are you so bent on shaming your father's house?

TEIRESIAS

When a sensible man
has a good cause to defend, to be eloquent
is no great feat. Your tongue is so nimble
one might think you had some sense, but your words
contain none at all. The powerful man
who matches insolence with glibness is worse than a
    fool.
He is a public danger!
This new God whom you dismiss,
no words of mine can attain
the greatness of his coming power in Greece. Young
    man,
two are the forces most precious to mankind.
The first is Demeter, the Goddess.
She is the Earth—or any name you wish to call her—
and she sustains humanity with solid food.

Next came the son of the virgin, Dionysus,
bringing the counterpart to bread, wine
and the blessings of life's flowing juices.
His blood, the blood of the grape,
lightens the burden of our mortal misery.
When, after their daily toils, men drink their fill,
sleep comes to them, bringing release from all their
troubles.
There is no other cure for sorrow. Though himself a
God,
it is his blood we pour out
to offer thanks to the Gods. And through him,
we are blessed.
You mock the legend
of his being stitched inside the thigh of Zeus!
Let me teach you how legends are born.
When Zeus snatched the infant God out of the flames
and lifted him to Olympus, Hera, his wife,
schemed to have him thrown out of heaven. But Zeus,
with typical God's wit, devised his own counterplot.
He tore some pieces off the sky that envelopes the
earth,
and presented them to nagging Hera
as the salvaged limbs of the child,
while he rushed the real Dionysus to safety.
Men, however, through retelling a story,
often wander from the truth. In time,
out of a mere play of words, grew this myth,
that the child had been salvaged *in* the limbs of Zeus.
This God is also a prophet. Possession by his ecstasy,
his sacred frenzy, opens the soul's prophetic eyes.
Those whom his spirit takes over completely
often with frantic tongues foretell the future.

His power even stretches to the realm of war.
You can see an army, positioned and ready for battle,
drop their spears and run for their lives
crazed out of their wits, by the grace of Dionysus.
A day will come when you shall see him
straddling the rocks of Delphi amid a blaze of torches,
leaping from peak to peak, swinging and hurling high
his thyrsus, the emblem of his glory
acclaimed throughout Greece. So Pentheus,
listen to me. Do not mistake the rule of force
for true power. Men are not shaped by force.
Nor should you boast of wisdom, when everyone but
        you
can see how sick your thoughts are. Instead,
welcome this God to Thebes. Exalt him with wine,
garland your head and join the Bacchic revels.
It's not for Dionysus to force women to be modest.
As in all things, moderation depends on our nature.
Remember this! No amount of Bacchic revels
can corrupt an honest woman.
Also, remember your own deep pleasure
when the crowds swarm outside your gates
and shout glory to your name.
Why should not *he*
be glad to have his name exalted?
I say he is.
So I—and Cadmus, whom you ridicule—
will wear our ivy crowns and will dance.
Old as we are, I promise you we'll dance.
And nothing you can ever say will make me
turn against the Gods. For you are sick,
possessed by madness so perverse, no drug can cure,
no madness can undo.

CHORUS

Your words, old man,
most wisely balance
respect for the Gods.
Without shaming Apollo
you honor our Bromius, as a great God.

[CADMUS *approaches* PENTHEUS, *carefully trying
to humor him*]

CADMUS

My boy, Teiresias has advised you well.
Stay close to us! Don't step outside the rules.
Just now you were up in the air, not thinking,
but thinking that you were. For even if you are right
and this God is not a God, why say it?
Why not call him one?
You have everything to gain from such a lie
that makes Semele, your aunt, the mother of a God.
Think what an honor for the whole family!
Remember Actaeon, my Actaeon, what a miserable
      end he came to—
my own grandson, torn limb from limb, in this very
      same valley
by the meat-devouring hounds that he himself had
      reared,
for the price of one boast: that he
was a better hunter than Artemis.
Don't risk the same fate. Here,
let me put this ivy on your head.
Join us in paying homage to Dionysus!

[PENTHEUS *swings around, knocking the thyrsus
out of* CADMUS' *hand. The old man staggers and
falls to the ground*]

Keep your hands off me! Go! Run to your Bacchic
   revels.
I want none of your senile folly
rubbing off on me! As for him,
your tutor in idiocy, I'll deal with him.
Run, someone, straight to this man's lair,
his rock of prophecy. Dig it up with crowbars,
topple it, tear the stones from their sockets,
smash it into dust.
Throw his holy emblems to the winds, the drunken
   winds.
That will sting him to the quick. The rest of you,
scour the city, find this effeminate stranger
who afflicts our women with this new disease
and who befouls our beds. And when you catch him,
drag him here in chains.
He'll taste the people's justice when he's stoned to
   death,
regretting every bitter moment of his fun in Thebes.

[*The* GUARDS *run off in several directions*]

TEIRESIAS

Poor fool! You don't know what you are saying.
You were out of your mind before. Now you are stark
   mad.
Come, Cadmus. The two of us will go and pray
both for this man—undeserving monster though he
   is—
and for Thebes, that the God might spare us all
from some new calamity. Take up your thyrsus
and follow me. Try to support me and I'll support you.
It would be a shocking sight, two old men

[21]

sharing one fall! But never mind. Anything
so long as Dionysus, son of Zeus, is served.
Oh Cadmus, Pentheus is another name for grief.
Watch over your house, for grief is stalking in his steps.
This is not prophecy but blatant fact.
You can tell a dangerous fool by his own words.

[TEIRESIAS *and* CADMUS *exit as* PENTHEUS *strides
into the palace*]

CHORUS

Holiness, power all transcending
soaring higher than the Gods
yet floating down on golden wings
to touch the earth, do you hear this man?
Do you hear the blasphemy
of Pentheus the unholy, hurled at Semele's son,
my Bromius, whom the garlanded Gods
when they feast on his bounty and his beauty
rate first among the first?

He is life's liberating force.
He is release of limbs and communion through dance.
He is laughter and music in flutes.
He is repose from all cares—he is sleep!
When his blood bursts from the grape
and flows across tables laid in his honor
to fuse with our blood,
he gently, gradually, wraps us in shadows
of ivy-cool sleep.

The unbridled tongue,
the arrogant frenzy of fools,
lead headlong to disaster.
But the tranquil life
of the wisely content

is anchored in rock and protects
the home from the storm.
The Gods may be far.
Yet, out of the hazy heavens,
they observe the ways of men.
Knowledge is not wisdom.
A knowing mind that ignores its own limits
has a very short span. And the man
who aims too high
never reaps what lies within his grasp.
Such is the folly—
and I know none worse—
of perversely ambitious, fanatical men.

Oh, to be in Cyprus,
the island-home of Aphrodite,
where the spirits of love
thrill the blood of men with magic breezes.
Or in that mythical land of the many-mouthed river
whose floods make deserts bloom.
Or where the muses play, Pieria,
whose peerless beauty
lovingly hugs the slopes of Olympus.
Oh, Bromius, my Bromius take me there!
Pave the way with romp and with prayer,
to the land of the Graces,
the land of Desire!
Where freedom is law
and women can revel with Bacchus.

The divine son of Zeus rejoices in festivity.
Of all his loves, the first is Peace,
the great benefactress
who cherishes the lives of young men.

He gives to the poor as he gives to the rich
the sorrow-killing drug of wine.
He hates only those who spurn
the daylight joys and the night's delights
that make life rich. How prudent
to keep one's heart and mind
away from those who think they know all.
Give me the simple wisdom and faith
of ordinary people. And I will make it mine.

[PENTHEUS *steps out of the palace, as several*
guards enter, leading DIONYSUS. *His hands are*
shackled]

GUARD

Pentheus, here we are. All that you asked is done.
We hunted down the prey you sent us out to catch.
An easy job, I have to own. You see,
the animal was tame, sir. Made no attempt to run,
just stood there, very friendly, holding out his hands.
He didn't flinch or lose that flush
of wine-glow in his cheeks, but always smiling urged us
to tie him up and turn him in. He even stepped right
     up—
to save me from the trouble. That made me feel
     ashamed
and I mumbled: "Look, stranger, this is not my doing.
I'm just a soldier carrying out the orders of the king."
But there is more. Those raving women
that you'd clapped in chains
and locked up in your prison—
well, sir, they're gone,
they're on the loose, prancing their way into the glens,
laughing and calling Bacchus, their chosen God.

The chains around their feet just fell apart,
the prison doors unbarred themselves,
untouched by human hand. If you ask me,
this stranger who has come to Thebes,
is capable of many miracles.
I had my say.
The rest is up to you.

PENTHEUS

Untie his hands.
Now I have him in my net, no amount of agile tricks
can help him slip away.

[*The* GUARDS *unshackle* DIONYSUS' *hands and step
aside, clearing the stage for the confrontation*]

So! You cut a handsome figure, I'll give you that!
Quite tempting—
I mean to women—the object, I don't doubt,
of your presence here in Thebes.
Your curls are soft!
A bit too long for wrestling, but very pretty
the way they hug your cheeks, so lovingly.
And what fair skin you have, so well looked-after!
But then, you don't expose it to the sun, do you?
You like the darker places,
where you can hunt desire with your beauty.
Now then! To start with, where are you from?

DIONYSUS

That's easy to answer, though nothing to boast of.
You must have heard of Mount Tmolus,
famous for its flowers.

PENTHEUS

So I have. It rings the city of Sardis.

DIONYSUS

I come from there. Lydia is my country.

PENTHEUS

Where did you learn these orgiastic rituals
that you bring to Greece?

DIONYSUS

Dionysus initiated me.
He is the son of Zeus.

PENTHEUS

Which Zeus? A native of those parts,
who coins new Gods?

DIONYSUS

No. The same Zeus who married Semele
in these parts of yours.

PENTHEUS

Did he possess you in your sleep
or by appearing to your eyes?

DIONYSUS

Face to face. He shared his mysteries with me.

PENTHEUS

What lies behind these mysteries, according to you?

DIONYSUS

That only the initiated may know.

PENTHEUS

And those who *are* initiated,
what are the benefits they gain?

DIONYSUS

You may not hear. Though you would gain by
knowing.

PENTHEUS

A crafty answer, baited to sting my curiosity.

DIONYSUS

Wrong. Our mysteries abhor the probing ears of
impious men.

PENTHEUS

This God you saw, or that you say you saw, what is he
like?

DIONYSUS

Like the likeness of his choice. Not mine.

PENTHEUS

Another devious answer and devoid of sense.

DIONYSUS

What makes no sense is talking sense to a fool.

PENTHEUS

Is this the first place to which you've brought your
God?

DIONYSUS

Throughout the Orient, people celebrate his dance.

PENTHEUS

I believe it. Next to the Greeks,
they're all barbarians.

DIONYSUS

In this, they're more civilized.
The standards differ.

PENTHEUS

Do you perform your mysteries
during the day or by night?

DIONYSUS

Mostly by night.
The dark is more conducive to worship.

PENTHEUS

You mean to lechery and bringing out the filth in
women.

DIONYSUS

Those who look for filth, can find it at the height of
noon.

PENTHEUS

You're going to pay for that rash, perverted mouth of
yours.

DIONYSUS

And you for being a crass and ignorant blasphemer.

PENTHEUS

Oho! Our Bacchus-fiend is getting bold!
Crossing swords with words, not bad!

DIONYSUS

Do tell me how you'll punish me.
What torture have you in mind?

PENTHEUS

First, I'll chop your dainty curls off. At the roots!

DIONYSUS

My hair is holy. I grow it long for God.

[*Unable to carry out his threat,* PENTHEUS *takes another tack, trying to reestablish his authority*]

PENTHEUS

Next, you'll hand that thyrsus over. Now!

DIONYSUS

Come and take it yourself.
I hold it in the name of Dionysus.

[DIONYSUS *holds out his thyrsus, but* PENTHEUS *cannot move. In his impotence, he flings empty threats at him*]

PENTHEUS

Last—I'll have you bodily removed.
I'll throw you in my dungeons.

DIONYSUS

The God himself will set me free. I only have to ask
him.

PENTHEUS

If you can get those raving bacchants to invoke him
with you,
perhaps he will materialize!

DIONYSUS

He's here now. He sees what is being done to me.

PENTHEUS

Where *is* he? To me he's quite invisible.

DIONYSUS

Where I am. Your lack of faith has blurred your vision.

PENTHEUS [*to the* GUARDS, *beside himself*]

Seize him! He's mocking me and he is mocking Thebes.

DIONYSUS

Let fools be warned. Place no chains on me.

PENTHEUS

And I say chain him. I am the only power here.

DIONYSUS

You do not know what your life is
or what you do, or who you are.

PENTHEUS

I am Pentheus, son of Echion. And Agave.

DIONYSUS

To boast of that name is to court your own doom.

PENTHEUS

Away with him!
Lock him up inside the stables, within my easy reach.
Let him wallow in the murky darkness that he loves
and dance his head off!
As for these women,
your fellow travelers and your accomplices in evil,
I'll either have them sold as slaves
or put their hands to different work. At my looms!
That will stop them thumping those infernal drums.

[DIONYSUS *holds out his hands, encouraging the*
GUARDS *to manacle them*]

DIONYSUS

I shall go. But nothing fateful, that is not my fate,
can come to me.
As for you, Dionysus himself, whose Godship you deny,
will call you to account for your outrageous conduct.
When you lay hands on me, it is *him* you put in prison.

[30]

[*The* GUARDS *lead* DIONYSUS *away*. PENTHEUS *exits*]

CHORUS

O Dirce, nymph of the sacred stream
sprung from the mighty river, Achelöus.
Once in your crystalline pools
you cradled the infant God,
snatched by Zeus, his father,
from the mouth of the living flame.
And the father cried: "Come, Dithyrambus,
born to be reborn from this male womb of mine!
I name you Bacchus. And Thebes
will someday know you by that name."
Why then, merciful Dirce,
when I come to you with garlands
and group-binding love, do you turn away?
Why do you spurn me? Hound me?
I swear by the clustered grape,
you will learn to care for him,
who is Bromius, great in the East.

What fury, what venomous fury
rages in Pentheus,
the earthborn and earthbound,
spawned by the sperm of the snake!
No man,
but a monster caged up in a man,
leaping through eyes of blood
to strike at the kill,
a vicious dwarf with giant dreams
pitting his strength against the Gods.
Soon, too soon, I fear

[31]

he will bind me with chains,
me, who am bound to Bacchus with freedom.
He has plunged my comrade,
my leader in the dance,
in the black depths of his dungeon.

Oh Dionysus, son of God,
do you see our sufferings?
Do you see your faithful
in helpless agony before the oppressor?
Oh lord, come down from Olympus.
Shake your golden thyrsus
and stifle the murderer's insolent fury.
Where are you, God?
Leading your band of revelers
through the wilds of Nysa,
haven of free-roaming beasts?
On the towering crags of Corycia?
Or in the secret glens of Olympus,
where Orpheus once, making music with his lyre,
gathered the trees around him,
gathered the spellbound beasts?

Oh happy, happy Pieria!
Bacchus honors you.
He will come to you with dances,
crossing the swirling torrents of Axios,
waving the whirling maenads on
across the mighty banks of Lydias,
bountiful father of rivers,
into that land of gushing waters,
blessed with the grace of its horses
and the fertile beauty of its pastures.

[*As the* CHORUS *falls silent, a voice is heard—
that of* DIONYSUS—*calling as if from the guts of
the earth. Agitated, the* CHORUS *scatters around
the stage*]

DIONYSUS

Io! Hear me! Oh, my bacchae!
Do you hear my cry? Io, my bacchae! Io!

CHORUS

Who calls? Where does it come from, this cry,
calling in the voice of Dionysus?

DIONYSUS

Io! Io! Again I cry to you—
I, the son of Semele and of Zeus.

CHORUS

Io, Io, lord! Our lord!
Come to us, come to your loving companions,
your group of worshipers.
Oh, Bromius, Bromius!

DIONYSUS

Earthquake almighty,
shake the floor of the world!

[*The stage grows dark. A low rumble is heard,
building in intensity, until everything seems to
be reeling. The* CHORUS *sways and stumbles,
crazed with fear*]

CHORUS

Ah, look!
The palace of Pentheus is trembling!
It's reeling! It will collapse!
Dionysus is within the walls! Kneel to him!

The stones of the pillars are cracking!
They're crashing to the ground!
Bromius is here! Blasting the roof with his laughter!

DIONYSUS

Let the blazing bolt of lightning strike!
Burn down the palace of Pentheus! Burn it down!

[*A flash of lightning is followed by a crash of thunder, and flames leap up from Semele's tomb*]

CHORUS

Ah! Ah!
Over there, do you see?
Look how the fire leaps
out of Semele's holy tomb!
How the lurking flame
left there once by the bolt of Zeus,
springs to life!
Down, trembling maenads. Fling your bodies to the
    ground.
He rises from the ruins
of the once-mighty house,
that he himself has laid to dust.
Here he comes, the son of God.

[*The women fling themselves to the ground, covering their heads. As the lights build up,* DIONYSUS *comes out of the palace and threads his way among them, helping them rise*]

DIONYSUS

Women of Asia, my barbarians!
Why are you cowering, trembling, on the ground?
I know! It seems you saw, as I did,
how Bacchus shook the palace of Pentheus.

But come! Rise to your feet.
Shed the fear from your limbs.

CHORUS

CHORUS

Light of lights, oh leader of our holy dance!
What joy to see your face!
Without you, I was lost.

DIONYSUS

Have you so little faith as to despair
the moment I was led to Pentheus' murky prison?

CHORUS

What else could I do?
Who would be there to protect me
if some misfortune came to you? But tell us,
how did you escape that godless man?

DIONYSUS

It was easy.
I freed myself without undue exertion!

CHORUS

But were your hands not shackled?

DIONYSUS

Ah! There I had him, made him look an utter fool.
All the while that he was thinking he was binding *me*,
me he didn't even touch! He fed on pure illusion.
You see, in the stable where he held me,
in strictest isolation, as he thought,
he came upon a bull and straightaway
tried to bind it by the hooves and knees.
He was panting with rage, sending showers of sweat
flying off his body, digging teeth into his lips,
while I sat quietly by and watched. Just then,

out of nowhere, Bacchus came and shook the palace,
setting his mother's tomb ablaze with flames.
Seeing this and thinking that the palace was on fire,
Pentheus went rushing around in circles,
shouting to his slaves to carry water from the river.
Every hand was put to the toil—for nothing!
Then, afraid I had escaped, he stopped his labors,
drew his sinister sword and charged toward the palace.
In that very instant, Dionysus—
I'm presuming it was he, I can but guess—
planted in his path a ghost,
uncannily resembling me.
Pentheus lunged at it, slashing the luminous air
and thinking with relish that he was killing me.
But that's not all the God had in store for him!
To demolish his pride even further,
he brought the palace crashing down onto the stables,
burying them beneath a heap of rubble, a sight to make
my imprisonment bitter to him.
Sheer exhaustion has now made him drop his sword.
He is prostrate—as any man should be,
who dares to wage a war with God.
As for me, I calmly walked out of the palace,
to join you here,
without another thought for Pentheus.
But wait! I think I hear his footsteps, stamping through
        the court.
His lordship threatens to emerge. I wonder what he'll
        say after this!
Let him stir up a storm. He shall not ruffle me.
A wise man knows restraint. His strength is his detach-
        ment.

[PENTHEUS *enters furiously*]

PENTHEUS

It's an outrage! He's got away! From *me*!
That stranger,
that man I'd clapped in chains.

[*He spots* DIONYSUS *among the* CHORUS]

Ha! There he is!
What is the meaning of all this?
How did you escape?
How dare you show your face outside my doors?

DIONYSUS

Get hold of yourself! Tread lightly or you'll trip.

PENTHEUS

How did you get here? How did you escape?

DIONYSUS

Did I not tell you—or did you not hear—
that somebody would set me free?

PENTHEUS

Who? Can you only talk in empty riddles?

DIONYSUS

He who makes the clustering vine
grow for mankind.

PENTHEUS

You mean he who drives our women from their homes!

DIONYSUS

For that splendid insult, I'm sure Dionysus thanks you.

PENTHEUS

Seal off the city.
Go around the towers and bolt all gates!

DIONYSUS

Whatever for?
Can't Gods jump higher than your city walls?

PENTHEUS

You're clever—very clever—
except where it counts.

DIONYSUS

It's where it counts the most that I am clever.
However, listen first to this man,
who comes from the mountains.
He brings you news!
We shall wait here. No, we shall not run away, I
   promise!

[*A* HERDSMAN *enters from the direction of Mount
Cithaeron. He is panting with fatigue and excite-
ment*]

HERDSMAN

Pentheus, ruler of Thebes, my king,
I come straight from Cithaeron,
leaving behind its craggy slopes, where dazzling snow-
   drifts
never melt!

PENTHEUS

That you've come, we know. Now get on with your
   message.

HERDSMAN

I saw them. The Bacchae. Those raving women
who, stung by holy frenzy, went darting off into the
     wilds
in a flurry of bare feet.
I couldn't wait to tell you, King,
you and everyone in Thebes, the weird,
the awesome things they do, miraculous beyond belief.
But, first, I want to know. Can I speak freely, frankly,
of their goings on, or must I trim my tongue?
Truth is, I'm a little scared of your lordship.
You're so impatient, so fierce of temper—
just like a king, only more.

PENTHEUS

Speak on. No matter what you tell me,
it's not you that I shall blame. Besides,
to penalize a man for telling you the truth,
is wrong. But the more harrowing your tale about the
     Bacchae,
the more crushing the punishment that I shall inflict
upon that man who put our women up
to these vicious new tricks.

HERDSMAN

The sun's first rays had just begun
to spill their warmth upon the earth,
and I was steering my cattle up the slopes
to the pastures near the ridge, when suddenly
I see three bands of women—resting from their dance.
Autonoe at the head of one,
Ino of another,
and Agave, your mother, of the third—all fast asleep,

wherever exhaustion had dropped them;
some with heads lying back on pillowy branches,
others stretched out on beds of matted oak leaves,
but modestly, serenely, sir, not the way you think.
They were not drunk with wine,
or seduced by the music of flutes,
so they'd be in raptures,
or chasing wild erotic pleasures in the woods.
But then, your mother, alerted by the lowing
of our horned bulls, sprang up,
and with a ringing cry urged the bacchae
to rouse themselves from sleep. And they,
shedding the bloom of sleep from their eyes, nimbly
     rose—
a sight miraculously orderly and graceful—
women young and old, and girls as yet unmarried.
First, they let their hair fall down their shoulders
and those whose fawnskins had come loose
fastened them up, while others girdled theirs
with snakes that licked their cheeks. Some,
mothers with newborn babies left at home,
cradled young gazelles or wild wolf cubs in their arms
and fed them at their full-blown breasts
that brimmed with milk.
Then they wreathed their heads with shoots
of ivy, oak and flowering bryony.
One of them lifted a thyrsus, struck a rock
and water gushed from it as cool as mountain snow.
Another drove a stick into the ground
and at the bidding of the God,
wine came bubbling up.
Those who wanted milk
just scratched the soil lightly with their fingers

and white streams flowed, while from their ivy-crested
     wands
sweet honey dripped like sparkling dew.
Oh, King,
if you had been there and had seen,
you would have offered grateful prayers to the God
you now denounce.
Well, we cowherds and shepherds of those parts
got together and discussed these marvels,
these awesome things we had witnessed.
And one of our crowd, one who's always sneaking up
     to town,
very smooth with words, held forth to us and said:
"You people living in these holy glens,
what do you say we hunt Agave out,
drag her away from her orgies and do a service to the
     king, her son?"
He talked good sense, we thought, so we hid ourselves
low among the thickets, waiting in ambush.
At a given hour, all the Bacchae
shook the thyrsus for the revels to start
and their voices joined into a single cry:
"Iacchus, son of Zeus, oh Bromius, evoë."
And the whole mountain reeled,
possessed by their ecstatic dance,
and the beasts too and the trees,
suddenly everything but everything
was on the move. Then, quite by chance,
Agave came whirling past me, and I,
leaping out from my cover in the bushes,
tried to seize her. But she called out, yelling:
"Come, my fleet-footed hounds!
We're being hunted by these men! Take up your thyrsus

and follow, follow me!" At this, we fled
and barely escaped being torn to pieces
by these God-struck maenads.
But our cattle—
our herds grazing on the grassy slopes—oh!
They fell upon them with their naked hands.
You could see a woman sink her nails into a cow,
with its udders full, and lift it, bellowing, high above
    her head.
Others dragged young heifers, ripping them apart.
Everywhere you looked,
ribs and cloven hooves
were flying through the air.
And from the pine branches
dangled lumps of flesh that dripped with blood.
    Majestic bulls,
one minute aiming their horns with all their furious
    pride,
the next were stumbling to the ground,
overwhelmed by the swarming hands of girls,
their bones stripped clean of all their flesh,
faster than you could blink your royal eyes.
Then, taking off with sudden speed, like birds,
they swooped down the hillside to the flatlands—
fattened with crops by the river Asopos—
and like a rampaging army they burst into the villages
that nestle in Cithaeron's foothills.
They ransacked everything in sight.
They snatched young children out of homes,
carried them on their shoulders along with other
    plunder
and everything stayed put, without being tied. Nothing,
not even bronze or iron, fell to the somber earth.

Flames flickered in their hair and did not burn them.
The villagers, enraged, of course, by all this havoc,
took arms against the Bacchae. Then,
what a spectacle, my king, how eerie!
Their pointed spears drew no blood,
while the women, just hurling the thyrsus,
opened wounds, the women, sir, turned men to flight!
That could not have been without some godly power.
They went back then
to the haunts from which they started,
those fountains which their God had sprung for them.
They washed their bodies clean of blood
and from their cheeks, the serpents licked away the
    stains.
Oh, my king, this God, whoever he may be,
is powerful in many things. It was he,
so they say, who gave to us, poor mortals,
the gift of wine, that numbs all sorrows.
If wine should ever cease to be,
then so will love.
No pleasures left for men.

CHORUS

It frightens me to speak
my free thoughts
freely in a tyrant's presence.
But let the truth be told:
Among the Gods, Dionysus is second to none.

PENTHEUS

So, it has come!
This Bacchic violence, this hysteria,
spreading like a raging fire, is already upon us.
We are disgraced in the eyes of all Greece.

This is no time for apathy. You!
Go to the Electran gate, run!
Call every able-bodied man to arms!
Mobilize the cavalry in full!
Everyone who can use a sling or spring a bow,
I want them all. We march against the bacchae.
It will be a black day indeed
when men sit back and endure such conduct from their
    women.

> [*The* GUARD *runs off. The* HERDSMAN *creeps out
> without being noticed.*
> DIONYSUS *turns to* PENTHEUS *and speaks to him
> soberly, reasoning with him, as if casting a spell*]

DIONYSUS

Pentheus, nothing I can say will move you, *that* I know.
Yet even so!
In spite even of the grievous wrong you've done me,
I shall warn you again. Do not take arms against a God.
Let things be. Dionysus will not let you
drive his Bacchae from their sacred mountain haunts.

PENTHEUS

I need no lectures from you.
You've escaped from prison once—relish that!
Or do you want me to send you right back?

DIONYSUS

If I were you,
I would offer him a sacrifice. Not angry threats,
which, you being mortal, he a God,
is just like kicking barefoot at a rock.

PENTHEUS

Sacrifice? Exactly what I plan to offer him.
Women's blood—most suitably supplied by his own
     victims.
I'll drench the glens of Cithaeron with it!

DIONYSUS

Unless you're routed. Which you will be.
The lot of you. Just think of the disgrace!
Your shields of bronze being beaten back by sticks of
     ivy!

PENTHEUS

This stranger's like a nightmare that you can't shake off.
Whether you ignore him or kick him, he will have his
     say.

DIONYSUS

Friend, it still is possible to put things right.

PENTHEUS

How? By making myself a slave of my slaves?

DIONYSUS

I shall bring those women back to Thebes
without the help of weapons.

PENTHEUS

Ha! This is another of your artful tricks.

DIONYSUS

A trick? Is using my power to save you a trick?

PENTHEUS

No. It's a conspiracy with them—those Bacchae—
so that you can revel on forever.

DIONYSUS

True. Conspiracy if you like—but with a God.

[PENTHEUS, *who has been steadily losing ground, wavers. Suddenly, breaking out of the spell, he springs away, yelling*]

PENTHEUS

My arms! Go fetch my arms.
And you stop talking.

DIONYSUS

Ah!*
How would you like to *see* them
all cooped up together in the hills,
having their orgies?

PENTHEUS

Would I? I'd pay a fortune in gold for that.

DIONYSUS

Why, what gives you such a passionate desire?

PENTHEUS

Mind you, I would be very sorry
to see them drunk. . . .

DIONYSUS

But for all your sorrow
you will be delighted to see them, will you not?

PENTHEUS

Oh, yes, very. I could crouch beneath the pines,
silently.

---

* This marks the turning point of the scene. Dionysus becomes wily and insinuating, drawing Pentheus deeper and deeper into his nets by bringing out his baser instincts.

DIONYSUS

However well you hide, they'll find you out.

PENTHEUS

That makes sense. I'll go openly! Of course!

DIONYSUS

Well, shall we go? You'll undertake the journey?

PENTHEUS

The sooner the better. I'll blame you for delaying me.

DIONYSUS

Wait! First you must dress yourself in something soft
and feminine.

PENTHEUS

What! I, a man, look like a woman?

DIONYSUS

If they see you as a man, they'll kill you.

PENTHEUS

You're talking sense again. Shrewd as an old wizard,
aren't you?

DIONYSUS

Dionysus tells me what to say.

PENTHEUS

Sensible as your suggestion is, how can I make it work?

DIONYSUS

I will come inside and dress you myself.

PENTHEUS

Dress me? In what—a woman's dress?
Oh no, I'd be ashamed.

DIONYSUS

I see! You're no longer keen to watch the maenads!

PENTHEUS

What exactly do I have to wear?

DIONYSUS

On your head, long flowing hair.

PENTHEUS

And then? What style of outfit do you have in mind?

DIONYSUS

Robes down to your feet and veils in your hair.

PENTHEUS

And to go with that? What else?

DIONYSUS

A dappled fawnskin and a thyrsus in your hand.

PENTHEUS

No, never!

DIONYSUS

Then fight with the bacchae.
And be ready for a bloodbath.

PENTHEUS

You're right.
It's good tactics to spy on them first.

DIONYSUS

Wiser and safer
than to invite violence by using it.

PENTHEUS

But how shall I pass through the city
without being seen?

DIONYSUS

We shall take lonely and deserted streets. I'll be your
    guide.

PENTHEUS

Anything, so long as I'm not jeered at by any of those
    Bacchae.
I need to think it over. I'll go in . . . and decide.

DIONYSUS

As you please.
I am prepared for all eventualities.

PENTHEUS

I leave you. I shall re-emerge,
either to lead my army to the mountains
or to fall in with your plans.

    [PENTHEUS *goes into the palace*]

DIONYSUS

Women, there goes a man walking straight into the net.
He shall visit the Bacchae
and there find punishment and death.
Dionysus, to your work. I know you are near.
Be revenged on this man.
But, first, unhinge his mind,
make it float into madness.
Sane, he never will accept to wear a woman's dress.
But once his wits have broken loose, he will.
I want the whole of Thebes to laugh
as I parade him through the streets,
laugh at this womanly man, this terrifying king,
whose arrogant threats still thunder in our ears.
I shall go to him. Time to deck him out

in the clothes he shall take with him to Hades,
slaughtered by his own mother's hands.
So shall Pentheus come to know Dionysus, son of Zeus,
a God sprung from nature, like nature most cruel,
and, yet, most gentle to mankind.

[DIONYSUS *follows* PENTHEUS *into the palace*]

CHORUS

When, oh when,
in an all-night trance
shall I dance again,
bare feet flashing, head rushing
through the coolness of leaves,
like a fawn that frolics
in the green delights of the forest,
free from the deadly snares of the hunt.
Oh, but till then,
the terror of leaping
clear of the intricate nets
and the pouncing claws of hounds
unleashed by the hunter's frenzied command,
fleeing like a shuddering breeze
over the marshlands, over the river,
to the sheltering arms of the forest
to exult as the thick-sprouting trees
close their shadows around it
in dark pools of solitude
empty of men.

What is wisdom? Which
of all the God-given gifts
is more beneficial to man

than the power to hold
an enemy powerless at bay?
That which is good is welcome forever.

Slowly, but implacably,
divine power moves
to strike at the arrogant man
who brazenly worships
his own image as God
and not the Gods themselves.
But they are there.
Above us, in us, around us
the Gods lie subtly in ambush.
At a point in time they pounce
on the impious man.
No mortal act, no human thought
shall trespass beyond the age-old truths,
fortressed by tradition and custom.
Faith costs little.
To believe in some essence supreme
is to believe in life;
to draw strength from whatever
is rooted in time
and in Nature's inscrutable logic.

What is wisdom? Which,
of all the God-given gifts
is more beneficial to man
than the power to hold
an enemy powerless at bay?
That which is good is welcome forever.

Happy the man who escapes
from the raging seas into port.

Happy the man who withstands
life's assaults.
Somehow, in some way, some man surpasses some
　　　other
in position and fortune.
For the millions of men there are millions of hopes.
For some, these ripen into happiness,
for others into nothing.
Count lucky the man who is happy on this one day.

[DIONYSUS *emerges from the palace. He turns and
calls to* PENTHEUS]

DIONYSUS

You, lusting to see what you are unfit to see,
thinking unthinkable thoughts,
you, yes you, Pentheus, come out.
Reveal yourself as a woman!
Let's see this maenad in her Bacchic dress,
who goes to spy on her mother and her friends.

[PENTHEUS *comes slowly out of the palace. He
wears a woman's dress and a veil over his long
golden curls, and he carries a thyrsus. He walks as
if in a trance, trying to keep his balance*]

Well! You look exactly
like one of Cadmus' daughters.

PENTHEUS

Strange! I seem to see two suns
and—two Thebes, yes,
two cities, two, each with seven gates. And you—
walking there before me—are you a bull?

I could wager that you are one,
with those horns
that have sprouted from your head!
Were you one before? An animal? I mean a bull,
decidedly a bull!

DIONYSUS

The God is with us. Though angry before,
now he's been placated and walks beside us graciously.
Now you see what you ought to see.

PENTHEUS [*posing narcissistically*]

How do I look? Like Ino,
or do I carry myself more like my mother, Agave?

DIONYSUS

Looking at you, I could swear I was seeing one of them.
Oh dear! One of your curls is out of place!
It should be tucked in as I arranged it.

PENTHEUS

It must have shaken loose indoors
when I was tossing my head, getting into a Bacchic
    mood.

DIONYSUS

Let me, whose job it is to serve your grace,
put it back in place! And hold your head still.

PENTHEUS

Come along then, fix it. I'm all yours now.

DIONYSUS

Your girdle too has slipped. And your skirt,
how unevenly it drapes around your ankles!

PENTHEUS

Yes, now I see it. At least on the right.
On the left, it hangs well to the heel.

DIONYSUS

You may think me your best friend yet
when, much to your surprise, you see how docile the
Bacchae are.

PENTHEUS

Do I hold the thyrsus in the right hand or the left
to be like them exactly?

DIONYSUS

In the right.

And swing it up as you swing your right foot forward.

[*He watches with wry amusement as* PENTHEUS
executes his instructions]

I do applaud the change in your mind.

PENTHEUS [*incongruously showing off his masculinity*]

Do you think I could lift the whole of Cithaeron,
Bacchae and all, upon my shoulders?

DIONYSUS

If you wished, you could. Before, your mind was
unsound.
Now it works the way it should.

PENTHEUS

Shall we take up crowbars?
Or shall I put my shoulder to the cliffs and wrench them
loose,
while my hands tear down the peaks?

DIONYSUS

It wouldn't do to wreck the playgrounds of the nymphs,
the groves where Pan sits piping!

PENTHEUS

You are right. It's demeaning to conquer
women by force. I shall hide among the pines.

DIONYSUS

You will hide where you must hide and you'll be
    hidden,
as well as any spy should be, when peeping on his
    fellow maenads.

PENTHEUS

I can see them now—crouched among the bushes
like mating birds, trapped in each other's loving arms.

DIONYSUS

Now we both know what you long to go and watch.
You may even catch them—if they don't catch you first.

PENTHEUS

Lead me through the very heart of Thebes.
Let them all see that I alone among them,
am *man* enough to dare.

DIONYSUS

You and you alone bear the burden for the city.
The struggle that awaits you is great.
Your destiny is unique.
Come. I shall take you safely there.
Someone else will bring you back.

PENTHEUS

You mean my mother!

PENTHEUS

In triumph! For everyone to see.

PENTHEUS

It is for that I go.

DIONYSUS

You will be carried home—

PENTHEUS

You thrill me!

DIONYSUS

—carried in your mother's arms.

PENTHEUS

Now you're spoiling me!

DIONYSUS

The way you *should* be spoiled. . . .

PENTHEUS

No less than I deserve.

[PENTHEUS *exits*]

DIONYSUS

Go, terrifying man, go your terrifying way
to the terror you'll be privileged to know,
the glory that will hoist you to the skies.
Stretch out your arms, Agave,
and you, her sisters, daughters of Cadmus.
I bring him! This man so young,
I bring him to his ultimate struggle.
The victory is mine. The victor Dionysus.
The event will tell the rest.

[DIONYSUS *exits*]

Run, swift hounds of madness, run,
run to the mountain,
find the faithful possessed,
the daughters of Cadmus,
goad them, lash them, turn them loose
on the woman-posing, woman-hating maniac
perversely spying in skirts.
His mother will spot him first,
through a crack in the rocks,
through a break in the trees.
She'll cry to the maenads:
"What creature is this, prowling on the hills,
prying on the Bacchae,
these hills, our hills, the hills of the holy revels?
Who bore him? A woman?
No woman's blood in such as him.
A gorgon's seed, whelped from a she-wolf."

Arrive,
come Justice, arise,
shining with the flash of your sword! And drive,
drive it clean through the throat
of the godless, lawless, ruthless son of Echion,
the earthborn, the earthbound.

Justice is balance.
His mind, unbalanced,
reels with sick, iniquitous passion,
profaning the mysteries of God,
lusting to violate Nature herself,
the Holy Mother.
On he goes, up he goes,
his fury outracing his madness

as he plunges towards the unassailable goal,
the matching of visible force with invincible strength.
He will die, as he must. It is the Law.
The invisible line drawn by the Gods
that no man can overstep.
Call it humility, acceptance, or just faith.
To know that our days are but as dust,
to be content with that and love each living particle,
is our only strength. But strength enough
to make our peace with grief.
Let others crowd their minds with scholarly wisdom.
Them I do not envy. I rejoice in keeping
my mind open to pursue the simple, attainable things
that are also the greatest.
Within that pursuit
lies the only known measure for happiness—
purity through loving by day and by night;
joyful acceptance of the godliness in me
which reconciles me humbly with the powers beyond.

Come Justice! Arise! Arrive,
shining with the flash of your sword. And drive,
drive it clean through the throat
of the godless, lawless, ruthless son of Echion,
the earthborn, the earthbound.

Come, God—
Bromius, Bacchus, Dionysus—
burst into life, burst
into being, be a mighty bull,
a hundred-headed snake,
a fire-breathing lion.
Burst into smiling life, oh Bacchus!

Smile at the hunter of the Bacchae,
smile and cast your noose.
And smiling, always smiling, watch
the maddened herd of maenads
burst upon him, bring him down,
trample him to death.

[*A* MESSENGER *arrives running from the direction
of Mount Cithaeron*]

MESSENGER

Oh, House, once happy throughout Greece!
Oh, envied race sown by Cadmus
in this Theban earth! I weep for you—
poor servant though I am!

CHORUS

What is it? Is there news from the Bacchae?

MESSENGER

Pentheus is dead. The son of Echion is dead.

CHORUS

Oh, Bromius, God of Joy! Yours is the glory!

MESSENGER

What did you say? Have you no shame, woman?
You rejoice at my master's misfortune?

CHORUS

I'm not one of you.
To you Greeks, I'm a barbarian from the East.
I speak my own language of worship.
I'm free from the fear of your chains!

MESSENGER

If you think the state of Thebes is short of men—

Dionysus, not Thebes, rules over me.
Dionysus is my state.

Well, I suppose one should excuse you.
But when disaster strikes
to jubilate after the fact is not decent.

Tell me all. Speak. What kind of death did he die,
the oppressor, the master of oppression?

After leaving the city,
we made our way through the farmlands
to the river Asopus, and, crossing it,
we struck into the foothills of Cithaeron—
Pentheus and myself, for I was escorting my master,
and that stranger who was acting as our guide.
Finally, we reached a wooded glen,
and now we paused, our voices hushed,
our footsteps muffled by the grass,
as we glided through the trees—to see and not be seen.
And there, looking down into a gorge,
sheer between two cliffs and full of streams,
we saw them, the maenads, quietly sitting
in the thick-knit shadows of the pines,
their hands aflutter with their happy tasks.
Some were dressing up their thyrsus
replacing old ivy with fresh green shoots.
Others, playful like colts, whose mouths
had just been freed from bridles, sang out in turn,
tossing their Bacchic tunes from throat to throat.

Pentheus—unhappy man—
somehow could not see all those women.
"Stranger," he said, "from where we stand
I cannot quite detect those so-called maenads.
But if I climbed the tallest pine tree on the ridge
I'd have a proper view of their obscene activities."
Then I saw the stranger work a living miracle.
Gripping the highest branch of a sky-piercing pine
he firmly bent it down, down,
down to the dark earth, till it arched like a bow,
as perfectly curved as a rim of wood,
flexed to hug the circle of a wheel.
So did the stranger arch that tree to the ground—
a feat no mortal hand could do.
Then, setting Pentheus astride the topmost branch,
he slowly let the sturdy trunk spring up again,
letting it glide smoothly through his grip,
so as not to throw him off.
Sheer into the sheer sky it went,
with my master riding on the top,
easier for the maenads now to see than he could them.
But barely had he risen into view
when the stranger was nowhere to be seen.
And a voice clanged through the mountain air—
that of Dionysus, I suppose—calling out:
"Women! I deliver unto you
the man who mocks at you and me
and at our holy mysteries. Now punish him!"
And as he spoke, a dazzling shaft of light
flashed between heaven and earth, binding them
        together.
The very air stood still. Throughout the glens, the trees

stifled the voice of their leaves
and in the hush, no beast was heard.
The Bacchae, who had heard the voice but not the
    words,
sprang up, their eyes and ears alert.
Then came the voice again. And now they knew,
Cadmus' daughters knew, the clear command of
    Bacchus.
Bursting forth, like a flock of racing doves,
Agave and her sisters and all the bacchae with them
up the cliffside, through the torrents,
over the boulders they leapt,
their limbs charged by the rage of their God.
And when they saw my master perched upon the pine,
first they scampered up a wall of rock,
across from where he soared, and pelted him with
    stones
and branches, stripped and hurled like spears.
Like hail they flung their sticks of thyrsus
at their pitiful target.
But still their aim fell short of the ill-fated wretch,
suspended on his dizzy perch,
beyond their furious reach, yet trapped without escape.
At last, like a bolt of forest lightning,
they struck an oak tree clear of branches,
and using them as levers,
tried to pry the pine tree from its roots.
But even then, their efforts failed. Agave then cried out:
"Maenads come, surround the trunk
and grip it with your fists.
Shake down this climbing animal
or he'll reveal the secrets of our holy dance."

A swarm of hands now swept upon the pine
and tore it from the earth. Then, plunging from the
	heights,
reeling toward the ground,
down, down, came Pentheus, with one continuous yell,
aware of his impending doom.
His mother,
as priestess of the ritual killing,
was first to fall upon him.
He stripped his head, tore everything away,
hoping that Agave, wretched woman,
would know him and not kill him.
He touched her cheeks and cried:
"No Mother, no, it is I,
your child, your Pentheus, born to you in Echion's
	house!
Have pity on me, Mother, I have wronged
but do not kill your son for my offense, not me, your
	son!"
She was foaming at the mouth.
Her eyes bulged, rolling wildly.
There was no corner of her mind
not possessed by Bacchus.
She was insane, oblivious to her son!
Seizing his left arm just above the wrist
and pushing with her foot against his chest
she wrenched his arm clean out of the shoulder.
It was not her strength that did it
but the God's power racing in her blood.
Ino, her sister, was working on the other side,
tearing off his flesh. And now Autonoe
pounced upon him, followed by the whole rabid pack.

The mountains boomed with shrill confusion—
Pentheus wailing while there was still a gasp left in him,
the women howling in their triumph.
One carried off an arm,
another a foot with the boot still on it.
They laid his ribs bare—clawed them clean.
His blood still warm on their hands,
they tossed the flesh of Pentheus back and forth
like children playing games.
Nothing is left of him. His body
lies scattered—some of it on the jagged rocks,
some buried in the forest thickets—
by no means easy to recover.
Except for his poor head. His mother has it,
proudly in her grip. She raises it high
on her thyrsus point—that head
she thinks is of some forest beast—
and carries it through the glades of Cithaeron,
leaving her sisters dancing with those raving women.
She is on her way here, inside the city,
exulting in her fearful and pathetic quarry.
She cries out to Bacchus, calling him
"fellow-hunter," "my ally in the kill,"
"the victor of our chase"! Oh, what a victory!
What a triumph of tears! But I am going.
I want no more part of this unnatural horror.
Just let me get away, far away,
before Agave comes home.
I am but a simple man, yet to me
reverence and humility before the Gods
is best for all men. It is also the only wisdom.
If only men would use it. So I think.

[The MESSENGER *exits, leaving the* CHORUS *in a state of fear and exultation]*

CHORUS

Dance for Bacchus,
dance.
Let voices boom
in song
for the doom
of Pentheus, seed of the dragon.
Pentheus,
dragged to his death
by the folds of his female dress,
pulled *down* into darkness
by the gentle thyrsus
he held so *high*.
Pentheus, the profane,
marched by a bull to his slaughter.
Oh Thebes! Oh Theban Bacchae!
What a victory you have won!
What a ringing triumph
to be drowned in wailing and tears.
Yet—salute one must
the horror and the glory
of the final reckoning,
that embrace of blood
between a mother and her child
that she herself has killed.
But look! I see Agave, Pentheus' mother,
running wild-eyed toward the palace.
Prepare yourselves
for the roaring voice of the God of Joy.

[AGAVE *enters, holding the head of* PENTHEUS. *Her dress is torn and there is blood on her hands and arms. She comes to a sudden stop as she sees the* CHORUS, *clinging to her trophy with jealous pride*]

AGAVE

Women of Asia, Bacchae—

CHORUS

Me? What do you want of *me*?

AGAVE

From the mountain, I have brought it.
All the way, a tender branch,
fresh-cut, with curly shoots. A beautiful catch.

CHORUS

We see. And we accept you.
We shall cry out together.

AGAVE

Without a trap, I trapped it.
A lion—a savage whelp of a lion.
Look! Look at it!

CHORUS

In what wilderness, how?

AGAVE

Cithaeron . . .

CHORUS

Cithaeron?

AGAVE

Killed him. Most totally.

CHORUS

But who, whose hands?

AGAVE

Mine first! Mine is the prize for striking first!
You know what the other women are singing?
Agave, the best. Agave, most blest.

CHORUS

Who else? Whose hands?

AGAVE

Oh, Cadmus' . . .

CHORUS

Cadmus!

AGAVE

Cadmus' daughters. My sisters,
yes, but only after me, after *me*,
did *they* lay hands on the quarry.
Oh, what a fortunate hunting.

CHORUS

The God knows when to smile.

AGAVE

Come feast with me. Share in my success.

CHORUS

Share—unhappy woman?

AGAVE

The beast is young! See how the down
blooms upon its cheek like newborn silk,
under the rich, soft mane.

CHORUS

The hair does make it look indeed
like a beast of the woods.

AGAVE

Bacchus,
skilled hunter that he is,
most skillfully unleashed his maenads
and led them to the kill.

CHORUS

God is the king of hunters.

AGAVE

Do you praise me?

CHORUS

We do—praise you.

AGAVE

So will Cadmus soon.
So will all his people.

CHORUS

And Pentheus?
Will he also praise his mother?

AGAVE

He *will* praise her
when he sees the lion she has caught.
Is it not glorious?

CHORUS

Prodigious.

AGAVE

Prodigiously conquered.

CHORUS

You rejoice?

AGAVE

More! I exult!
My conquest is great, plain to see!
And great the acclaim it deserves.

CHORUS

Show then, poor woman, show to everyone in Thebes
this priceless trophy you have carried proudly home.

[AGAVE *parades the stage, proudly exhibiting the head of* PENTHEUS]

AGAVE

You, people of this high-towered city,
subjects of this mighty country, look!
Here is my trophy! *Here* is the quarry
we, your women, hunted down, yes *we*—
and not with nets or hooks or pointed spears—
but with our own bare arms, our hands, our delicate
        fingers.
Now what are they worth, your manly boasts?
Where *is* the pride in power that relies
on hideous tools of war? *We* didn't need them.
With our hands we captured this beast of prey
and ripped it limb from limb.
But where is my father?
He is old, but he should come.
And Pentheus, my son,
where is he? Fetch him, someone. Tell him
his mother wants him. With a ladder.
He shall set it up against the front

of his palace. Firmly—for he musn't slip—
and nail high upon the highest wall,
so all the town can see
his mother's triumph in the hunt,
this lion's head, my trophy, yes *mine*!

[CADMUS *enters, followed by attendants carrying a
makeshift stretcher with the covered remains of*
PENTHEUS. *They remain upstage while* CADMUS
speaks]

CADMUS

Come men, follow me.
Bear your pitiful burden
of that which was Pentheus, my Pentheus,
to his home. Follow me with—
oh, those broken limbs that I painfully assembled
after a long and dismal search
up in the glens of Cithaeron, where they lay
scattered far and wide among the forest crags,
in tiny fragments, hard to find.
I had already left the mountain revels
and was entering the city with Teiresias,
when news was brought to me
of my daughters' atrocious deed.
I hurried back to the hills, to return, this time,
with this boy, dismembered by the maenads.
There on the wooded slopes I saw Autonoe,
my poor Actaeon's mother, and with her Ino,
both still possessed with frenzy. But Agave, I was told,
was seen running, raving, on her way here.
Oh! Too true, alas, I see her now.
A sight to make eyes bleed!

AGAVE

Father!
Be proud! As proud as any mortal man can be.
For you have sired the bravest daughters ever
in the world. I mean all three of us,
but me above the rest. From now on,
no more weaving at the loom, no little chores for me.
I'm meant for greater things—for hunting
savage beasts with my bare hands.
Oh Father, you see what I carry in my arms?
It is the prize I have won—yours,
to hang upon your walls.
Receive it, Father, in your hands. Rejoice in my
        conquest,
and summon all your friends to join our royal feast.
Let them see how fortunate you are. How blest
by the splendor of my deed.

CADMUS

Oh misery, oh grief beyond all measure.
I cannot look on this, this—murder—
yes, murder, done by those pitiful hands you're so
        proud of!
And you would offer such a victim to the Gods,
expecting Thebes and me to sit in at your feast?
How just—yet how unfair—the price the God
had made us pay. Dionysus, lord of joy,
born of our blood, has cruelly laid us low!

AGAVE

How disagreeable old men can be!
Why does he look so mournful?
I wish my son would emulate his mother!

Go hunting in the wilds with the young men of Thebes
and outshine them all!
But all he knows, that boy, is how to fight the Gods.
He should be scolded, Father! Yes!
And you're the one to do it. Well?
Is no one going to fetch him,
to see me in my happiness?

CADMUS

Oh daughter, daughter!
If ever you come out of this and know what you have
   done,
you'll suffer pain insufferable. And if your mind
remains forever drugged against reality,
your happiness, being all delusion, is but the greatest
   misery.

AGAVE

What is there that is wrong?
Why all this talk of misery?

[*Making a decision,* CADMUS *approaches* AGAVE
*and talks to her with low intensity, trying to pull
her out of her trance*]

CADMUS

Listen to me! Do as I say.
First, look up at the sky.

AGAVE

I'm looking. What am I supposed to see?

CADMUS

Is it the same as always?
Or does it seem changed to your eyes?

AGAVE

It is brighter than before—more luminous.

CADMUS

And inside you?
Is there still that lightness? Like floating?

AGAVE

I do not grasp your meaning.
Yet—I feel different somehow. More—awake.
As if—something has shifted in my head.

CADMUS

Do my words reach you now?
Can you answer clearly?

AGAVE

Yes, but I forget.
What were we talking of, Father?

CADMUS

When you reached womanhood,
whose house did you marry into?

AGAVE

You gave me to a man of our Theban dragon-race.
His name was Echion.

CADMUS

In your husband's house—you bore a son.
Who was he?

AGAVE

Pentheus. Echion's son and mine.

CADMUS

And whose face is that
you're holding in your hand?

AGAVE

A lion's—so the hunting women say. . . .

CADMUS

Now look straight at it.
There's little effort in that.

AGAVE [*turning her head away*]

Ah! What is this! What am I holding?

CADMUS [*grasping her head, forcing her to look*]

Look at it! Go on looking
till you know what it is!

AGAVE

I see—oh, Gods, no, not this grief,
not this agony . . .

CADMUS

Does it seem like a lion now?

AGAVE

No. It is Pentheus—his head—
in my hands.

CADMUS

We wept for him
long before you knew.

AGAVE

Who killed him?
How did he come into my hands?

CADMUS

Oh, merciless truth—you always come too soon.

AGAVE

Tell me! Now! My heart is leaping out
to the horror I must hear.

CADMUS

It was *you*! You and your sisters!
You killed him!

AGAVE

Where? Where did he die?
Here at home? Or where?

CADMUS

In those same glens where Actaeon
was torn to pieces by his hounds.

AGAVE

Cithaeron? Why?
What evil fate drove him there?

CADMUS

He went to mock the God
and you, his Bacchic revelers!

AGAVE

But we? How did we get there?

CADMUS

You were driven mad.
The whole town was possessed.

AGAVE

Now I see it all.
Dionysus! He destroyed us.

CADMUS

You denied his deity,
reviled his name in public.

[*A pause. The violence of their despair ebbs into a quiet but piercing grief*]

AGAVE

Father, where is the body
of my beloved son?

CADMUS

Here! I have brought it home,
broken, painfully retrieved.

AGAVE

Broken? But are his limbs together,
decently composed?

CADMUS

What human hands could do,
ours did. Not much.

AGAVE

Oh, if only mine could undo what they have done.

CADMUS

Too late. When guilty people are struck mad,
their madness knows no guilt.

AGAVE

My guilt—my madness, yes!
But what did Pentheus have to do with that?

CADMUS

He was like you, contemptuous of the God.
And in a single devastating blow, the God

has brought us down, your sisters, you, this boy—
ruining my house and me. I had no son,
no male heir of my blood but him,
sprung from your unhappy womb! And now he's
     gone—
abominably, shamefully cut down—
he who was the pillar of my house.
Oh, my child, my king, my grandson,
our guiding light you were,
the keeper of our future.
This city held you in its awe. When you were near,
no man would dare to slight this gray old head,
for fear of you. And now I, Cadmus the great,
who sowed the Theban race and reaped a glorious
     harvest,
must go away, dishonored, an outcast from my home.
Oh, dearest one—to me as dear in death,
as when you were in life—
never again will you touch my face
and call me Grandfather and hug me in your arms and
     say:
"Has anybody done you wrong? Has anyone upset you,
made you sad? Just tell me who
and, Grandfather, I'll punish him myself."
And now you're gone, as miserably dead
as I'm alive, your mother broken,
none of us left but torn by grief.
If there be any man who challenges or scorns
the unseen powers,
let him look on this boy's death and accept
that which is God.

I grieve for you, Cadmus.
Though your grandson's punishment is just.
For you it is too cruel.*

AGAVE [*In a strange, almost impersonal voice*]

Father,
you see this woman
standing where I do.
She is your daughter.
Yet nothing is there left of what she was.
In one quick stroke, her hands,
blind and driven by the Gods,
have split her life in two.
Whatever was before
has crumbled, vanished,
behind a wall of blood.
For her—for me—
there's only now. An endless now,
stretching like a dark and empty desert
without past or future.
My son is dead. His mother killed him.
I am his mother. Those few words contain
horror, shame, anguish so immense
that no living creature should be able to endure.
Yet I live. How or why, I do not know.
And no longer do I ask to understand. For, if I do,
I might sin again and be denied the one last favor
that would be any mother's right to ask.

* From this point until the appearance of Dionysus in his divine
dimension—on page 82—there is a break in the manuscript. My
reasons for reconstructing the missing scenes in this particular
way are set out in my introduction.

CADMUS

What it that, my daughter?

AGAVE

To prepare my son for his journey to the dead.
He cannot go like this! I know my hands are cursed,
polluted with blood of my blood,
yet whose but mine can make whole again
that body that they proudly reared to manhood?

CADMUS

Oh, daughter! The holy laws forbid the ones who kill
to care for their victims.

AGAVE

My victim? Yes! But, Gods, I DID NOT KNOW!
If my son deserved to die and I deserved to kill him,
you've had your way! A little charity is all I ask!
To be allowed to wash him clean of blood with tears
and sing a dirge for every broken limb!
Oh, Father, spare me a little of the pity
that the Gods must feel for you.
Just let me put my son to sleep—
and let the Gods do what they want with me.
Punish me with death or life, I do not care!

[CADMUS *signals to the attendants, who approach
slowly with* PENTHEUS' *remains*]

CHORUS

Bring forth your sorrowful burden.
Do what you can, my daughter.
But do not linger more than it is seemly.
And steel your heart against a sight
hard for any mortal eyes to bear,
but most of all a mother's.

[The attendants stop near AGAVE. *During the following lines, she sets* PENTHEUS' *head next to his mangled limbs, caressing them as she laments on her knees]*

AGAVE

Put him down.
Oh, my child! My son!
Your mother's here
to heal your wounds and give you back your beauty,
that she herself reduced to . . . this! Oh no!
Proud head
that not so long ago these hateful eyes reviled
and now drench with tears. Rest where you belong.
    Remember
how once you nestled in my arms?
Oh dearest face—tender cheek, so young—
sweet mouth that suckled at my breast,
now forever closed. If you could speak,
what would you say to wrench your mother's heart,
that I have not already said a thousand times!
Oh my prince!
These noble limbs that soon I should have dressed
for some young girl, your bride,
how lifeless now they lie—
unnaturally, mercilessly mangled—
Oh I cannot! Help me!
No, no—I must be strong. Go someone, bring a shroud
fit for the burial of this king, my son.
My eyes shall not betray him with weakness.

[CADMUS takes off his cloak and approaches AGAVE]*

CADMUS

Here, my daughter,
take this old man's cloak. And come away.

AGAVE

Yes, Father. A little while and I am done.

[*ceremoniously holding the cloak over* PENTHEUS'
remains]

I wash your wounds.
With this princely shroud I cover your head.
I bind your limbs with love,
flesh of my flesh,
in life as in death,
forever.

[AGAVE *covers the remains with the cloak. In the
hush, the* CHORUS *sounds drained and disoriented*]

CHORUS

O Dionysus,
we feel you near,
stirring like molten lava
under the ravaged earth,
flowing from the wounds of your trees
in tears of sap,
screaming with the rage
of your hunted beasts.

How terrible your vengeance against those
who harness your forces
to their laws of unnatural order.
A free and open mind
is safe against the excesses
lurking in the secret juices of your plants.

But those who try to strangle you
in the roots of their own nature,
who oppress and are oppressed,
through you, achieve their own destruction.

[DIONYSUS *appears, suspended in space above the palace, as the bull-horned God*]

DIONYSUS

Hear me all! I speak to you now as Dionysus,
a God revealed to mortal eyes.
I came back to this land of my virgin birth,
to suffer the indignities that only human folly can
invent.
I was mocked at, chained, thrown in prison. Men like
Pentheus
who abuse their power in defiance of the Gods
shall ever rediscover the inexorable terror of divine
justice.
Now you, his kin, were made to kill the tyrant that you
gloried in.
You are unclean. And you shall go your separate ways,
leaving Thebes forever, to rid it from the curse of your
pollution.
Had you been willing to be wise when you had all,
today, instead of losing all, you would be thriving
allies
of the son of Zeus, your friend.

CADMUS

Spare us, Dionysus. We have sinned.

DIONYSUS

Too late to know me now. You did not when you
should.

AGAVE

We were wrong and we confess.
But you are merciless!

DIONYSUS

I am a God.
And when insulted, Gods do not forgive.

AGAVE

The Gods should be above the passions of mere men.

DIONYSUS [*in a distant, tired voice*]

So it was ordained from the beginning
by the almighty father, Zeus.

AGAVE

It is decided, old man. Give up.
The cruelty of the Gods demands our banishment.

DIONYSUS

Then go. Why delay the inevitable.

[AGAVE *and* CADMUS *begin to cross the stage,
moving in opposite directions*]

CADMUS

Oh child, what a terrible fate has overtaken us,
you, your sisters, and your wretched father.
A derelict old man, I'm doomed to live,
despised, in foreign lands. For sufferings like mine
there is no respite ever. Even when I sail
down the silent river to the world of the dead
I shall find no rest.

AGAVE

I shall live, Father. Alone, deprived of you.

[83]

[*As* AGAVE *and* CADMUS *pass each other, she turns and embraces him*]

CADMUS

Poor child,
why do you fold your arms around me,
like a swan sheltering its useless, old father?

AGAVE

Where am I to go? Cast out, unwanted,
whom can I turn to?

CADMUS

I do not know, my daughter.
Your father cannot help you.

AGAVE

Farewell, my home. Farewell, my city.
I leave you for exile. My once bridal bed
I leave you for misery.
Father, I weep for you.

CADMUS

Strange! I still feel pity
for you and for your sisters.

AGAVE

Brutal! Brutally ruthless the fate
Dionysus hurled at your house.

DIONYSUS [*fading away*]

Yes. And ruthlessly brutal the way
you dishonored his name in Thebes.

AGAVE

Farewell, my father.

CADMUS

Poor child, farewell.
Oh words—how futile you can be.

AGAVE

Take me, someone, to my sisters,
my pitiful sisters, that I must lead to exile.
I want to go far,
out of the sight of cursed Cithaeron
and Cithaeron out of my sight.
To a place no thyrsus threatens—or haunts
even in memory. Let those who wish,
be Bacchae after me.

CHORUS

The Gods take many forms.
They manifest themselves in unpredictable ways.
What we most expect
does not happen.
And for the least expected
God finds a way.
This is what happened here today.